Fluttering their way into my head

ALSO AVAILABLE FROM EVERTYPE

Éist leis an gCruinne
(Gabriel Rosenstock, 2014)

The Partisan and other stories
(Gabriel Rosenstock, illus. Mathew Staunton, 2014)

The Naked Octopus: Erotic haiku in English with Japanese translations
(Gabriel Rosenstock, illus. Mathew Staunton, 2013)

I Met a Man from Artikelly: Verse for the young and young at heart
(Gabriel Rosenstock, illus. Mathew Staunton, 2013)

Fluttering their way into my head

An exploration of Haiku
for young people

Gabriel Rosenstock

Translated from the Irish by
Mícheál Ó hAodha
with additional material by the author

evertype

2014

Published by Evertype, Cnoc Sceichín, Leac an Anfa, Cathair na Mart, Co. Mhaigh Eo, Éire. *www.evertype.com*.

First edition 2014.

A shorter version of this book was published in Irish as *Haiku, más é do thoil é* (Baile Átha Cliath: An Gúm, 2014, ISBN 978-1-85791822-9).

A catalogue record for this book is available from the British Library.

ISBN-10 1-78201-088-2
ISBN-13 978-1-78201-088-3

Typeset in Minion Pro, **Frutiger**, and Hiragino Kaku Gothic by Michael Everson.

Cover design by Mathew Staunton.

Printed and bound by LightningSource.

Contents

Part 1
The journey begins

Part 1
The journey begins

What age are you? In your teens? You're only beginning life's journey! One day, haiku master Issa was out walking when he spotted a wild goose. He didn't have to spot it. It was there in front of him. He had a little question for the goose, for himself:

> wild goose
> where did your journey
> begin?

Just three lines long. (Or short!) Three lines; and yet a haiku can contain a whole world. A world full of mysteries and new beginnings. So, tune in!

Issa had no idea where that wild goose had first set out on her long trip—or when. Nor could he know how her trip might end. All he could say with any certainty was: hey, there's a wild goose here in front of me now. I wonder where she came from?

Where did *your* journey begin? Where or when will it end? Maybe it never began. Maybe it will never end. Now, there's a thought!

Issa takes a good look at the goose. It's the heart that sees. And the heart can see far and wide, farther than eyes can see. This is haiku. Tuning in. Opening your eyes (and your heart) to what is. Observing what you see before you. Taking it all in, with as many of the senses as possible. Watching. Listening. Feeling. A haiku may be small in size but it can grow in your heart. Haiku is all about looking, looking and seeing, looking outward and inward, above and below, with all your heart. Does it sound like hard work? It's a joy. And if you don't believe me, read on.

Open your heart. Something is bound to jump in. A frog! A goose! All the miracles of life, big and small, fat and skinny, smooth and hairy, sweet-smelling, foul! Observe them carefully, as if for the very first time. Or the last. Let them amaze you.

Here's something new you could try: bow your head, in reverence, before reading each haiku. This gives it the sacred space it deserves!

Sensing the wonder of it all and getting it down in three lines, that's what haiku is about. It can become a way of looking at life, calmly, intensely. The best way to write haiku? Read the masters! Tune in!

So, this is what haiku is, a brief note about some aspect of the natural world of which you and I are a part. A vital part! Nature—a world that is constantly changing from one day to the next, from one season to the next. *You* are changing too, aren't you? Certainly! Everything that lives is subject to change. Water changes into steam, or vapour, doesn't it? And when vapour rises into the air, it eventually forms clouds. The wind blows, the clouds move. They grow dark and heavy. Rain falls.

A haiku is a form of rest, a brief rest during which we can take note of all the movement that's going on; we can move with it, like a cloud, or become utterly still.

The wild goose stopped for a little while. To take a short rest. Or maybe to have a bite to eat. And they meet, Issa and the goose. They look each other in the eye.

> wild goose
> where did your journey
> begin?

Where? How? When? Why? We can ask ourselves all of these questions and more. The haiku is not closed. It's open, as open as your eyes, your ears, your heart. Keep them open. That's what haiku says.

Issa addresses the goose. He confronts the goose. So must we. Life must be addressed, confronted, examined, questioned, tasted and enjoyed! This is what the haiku masters tell us: do not get entangled in dreams, do not try to escape from life. Tune in! Engage with life, to the full.

❀

No beginning, no end

A haiku does not begin with a capital letter. Why is this? It has no real beginning or end. A bit like the goose. We arrive on the scene not knowing where the goose has been, what she's been up to, or where she's going.

The haiku is modest. It doesn't want to attract too much attention to itself—no capital letters, no title, no rhyme. All the attention is focused on the goose. It's the goose that matters.

Where did you come from, goosey? This is the fundamental question that Issa poses here. It's a simple enough question, isn't it? Where did *we* come from? You and me. Where are we going?

Issa looks at the goose. So should we. If we're lucky enough to see a wild goose. Many people do not see what is there before their very eyes. Not only that, they do not see what's to the left or the right of them, above or below. Haiku can teach you how to do this, how to take note of what you see—all the lovely details, the shapes, smells, colours, textures and sounds of the natural world. Later on, you will be grateful to haiku for presenting you with this gift—to be able to see and appreciate much more of the world we live in—see it, smell it, touch it, feel every aspect of it! In this way, we become more alive and our spirits soar! On the wings of the wild goose!

Issa does not describe the wild goose. He doesn't need to, does he? He leaves that to us, to our imagination.

A goose that left its mark!

Issa wrote loads of haiku about geese. All types of birds had great charm for him—sparrows, cormorants, crows, cuckoos. You name it. He observed them closely and saw how hawks sometimes capture small birds and sit on them to keep their bottoms warm! It's a fact! Then they let them loose in the morning!

Here's another goose:

> before leaving
> the wild goose
> makes a big poo!

There's an old saying in Irish: *Nuair a chacann gé, cacann siad go léir*: "When one goose does a poo, ah sure—they all do!"

Look out for two things in haiku—stillness and movement. There was quite a big movement in the above haiku. A bowel movement!

Issa delighted in the coming and going of geese. This is what life is all about, coming and going. Everything is coming and going all the time, days, nights, seasons, people. Coming and going. All is flux, that's how a wise Greek called Heraclitus explained it long ago:

> thinking of leaving?
> goosey on her tippy-toes—
> tippy-toes!

That's lovely, that is! Can you see it? She's just about to take off. What he describes could have happened today, or yesterday. It's still fresh. That's a sign of a good haiku. We can sense the life in it, in the haiku, in Issa, in the goose—all the energy that is needed to take off and fly! Haiku, being so compact, is bursting with energy.

"Plainness and oddness", as Bashō said, these are the bones of haiku. Plain everyday things can often be a little odd, too, in their own way. A goose on her tippy-toes!

❀

How many miles can a wild goose fly in a day, do you think? Find out! How long does a goose live for? Any idea? Ten years? Fifty? There is so much we don't know. We press a button and we get an answer but that answer is never going to be as good as the answer we discover ourselves, by living, and feeling, and looking around and seeing what's going on.

Lightness of heart

Another day, Issa spotted a butterfly:

a light heart
flying through this life
a pale blue butterfly

Is he talking about himself? Is this the way to live, to have a light heart, float silently through this world like a butterfly, never to get bogged down? Would you like to live like that? It's up to you! You can be a butterfly or a bull in a china shop!

Geese! Butterflies! What next? A lot! In this book you will meet many animals and birds and all sorts of plants and insects! That's a promise! Once you've read and re-read the haiku in this book you will have gained a new-found respect for every aspect of the natural, living world—small insects, beetles, worms, snails, things that slither and hop and fly! Haiku will keep you alert and you'll be careful not to trample on living things or squash them when you are out walking or playing. You'll become more aware of Nature and all creatures great and small.

You will also begin to notice that everything in this world has its place in the great chain of being. You are one link in this great endless chain. We are all part of an invisible chain—you, me, Issa!

In 1804, he composed the following:

being blown forward
and forward ...
a tiny butterfly

See again—it's the heart that sees. A very simple haiku indeed, and yet very mysterious at the same time. The butterfly is not flying, it's being blown forward on the wind. To where? We do not know. You might as well ask the goose!

The boxer Muhammad Ali described his fighting style with these words: 'Float like a butterfly, sting like a bee.' We do not say *'like* a butterfly' or *'like* a bee' in haiku. It's simply the butterfly. Simply the bee. And we can write or read hundreds of haiku about them, all slightly different, all mysterious and unique in their own way.

This one, by Kyoshi, who lived much later than Issa, is one of my favourite butterfly haiku:

a butterfly
the sound as he eats—
so quiet!

Kyoshi! Now he was tuned in! It's not surprising to know that he wrote over 40,000 haiku! Three lines. That's all. We've got it all wrong when we think bigger is better. Here's a quote to chew on:

"Sometimes", said Pooh, "the smallest things take up the most room in your heart." —A.A. Milne

Tune into silence

It's hard to distinguish between stillness and motion in Kyoshi's butterfly haiku. They are almost intermingled. Do you feel quiet after reading it? Haiku can have this effect on people. It's necessary to be quiet now and again. The best haiku come to us when we are tuned into silence.

What is your favourite haiku so far? Make a card! Write: MY FAVOURITE HAIKU on it. Write out the haiku you like and draw a little picture to go with it; then send the card to someone who might like to hear from you and to read your favourite haiku!

Wandering here and there

Where did the wild goose come from? Where is she going? For that matter, where and how did the butterfly emerge? In times gone by, wandering was normal for many *haijin* (or haiku masters). Wandering and rambling meant that they did not become attached to any one place or community. If you are not attached to any one place or community, it means you can devote more time to the spirit—the spirit of haiku! They wandered the countryside moving from place to place—just as a cloud or a butterfly is carried lightly on the breeze.

Issa composed more than one hundred haiku on the subject of butterflies. Here's one you might like:

drinking tea alone—
each day
a butterfly comes to visit

Picture Issa enjoying a cup of tea. The little bubble in the cup of green tea *(issa)*—the cup of tea which was his own pen-name—the little bubble winks at him. He looks up and sees that his daily visitor has arrived again. A dancing butterfly. I wonder was it the same butterfly as the one described earlier, blown ever onwards by the breeze?

A butterfly could appear to him at any time of the day, in translation by David G. Lanouwe:

a butterfly emerges
and flies away...
morning moon

A lovely example of motion and stillness. These are natural apparitions that Issa describes but often they seem like supernatural apparitions, coming and going mysteriously.

By appearing together, butterfly and morning moon, the fleetingness of all things is brought home to us: they will always be there, hopefully, butterflies and the moon, but very often their appearance lasts only for a short while. And then they are gone. But not forever!

It was written in 1808. Robert S. McAdam was born in that year. Who was he? See if you can find out something about him. Honoré Daumier, a French artist, came into this world. The importation of slaves into the United States was banned. Issa noticed the brief appearance of a butterfly. Can we mention all these things in the same breath? Why not?

In haiku, every event is big, or small, depending how you look at it. One thing is for sure: in the world of haiku, there is no such thing as an insignificant event. Once you realize this, once you tune into the aliveness of the world and the fact that everything is significant, it can change your life. Really!

Tuning in means you allow the world to come into your life, into your head, into your spirit. It can happen instantly, or gradually. Here's a lovely example from the year 1820, again in translation by David G. Lanouwe:

fluttering their way
into my head...
plum blossoms

When we go to school, we learn that certain things are important and other things are not. But everything is important! Cromwell is a hero in England and something of a devil in Ireland. Churchill is a great hero in Britain but not so loved in India. Do we have to take sides? Do we have to look at people and events from one perspective only? Haiku teaches us to be less judgmental, not to take sides, to tune into the world and all nations, be universal, see our brother and sister in every living being and, like St. Francis, to see one life flowing in all things. Then you become more aware of the gift of life flowing in your own being. And that's good. Good for you. Good for the world. Let those plum blossoms in!

How often have you said, 'I'm bored!' How often have you heard other people with the same complaint? Once you awake to the world of haiku, boredom becomes a thing of the past. For people who read and write haiku, life is brimming with light and shade, with energy and colour and tastes and feelings and sounds and smells, changing from moment to moment, from season to season. Who could possibly be bored! Blossom!

When I first began to read haiku—goodness gracious, I must have read tens of thousands of haiku in the past forty years!—I used to feel sad when certain *haijin* pointed out how things emerge and then quickly vanish. Like a mirage! But later, my sadness melted. I understood that a butterfly would not be a butterfly if it did not flit here and there and disappear! Father Anthony de Mello said:

'Whatever is truly alive must die. Look at the flowers; only plastic flowers never die...'

Hold that thought! But don't hold it too long.

a butterfly emerges
and flies away...
morning moon

Many haiku have what is called (in Chinese) *yu wei* or an aftertaste. Keep a note of those haiku in this book (or wherever else you come across haiku), haiku which leave a little aftertaste behind! In the following butterfly haiku from the year 1818, when the butterflies leave it seems that the whole neighbourhood knows about it and feels the loss:

> butterflies depart—
> even the pines
> seem to know

So it goes. OK, two more butterfly haiku before we say goodbye—for a while. This one from the American master, J. W. Hackett, whose work I admired so much that I invited him to Ireland and translated some of his haiku into Irish:

> they come separately
> and then leave the garden as one
> giant butterfly

Back to Issa:

> it's all yours
> butterfly, rest yourself
> there on that mushroom

Motion dissolving into stillness.

We all need a break now and again. Reading or writing haiku is like having a rest because time slows down and stands still. The butterfly takes a siesta on one of the mushrooms and we rest with it for a spell.

There's no adjective in that last haiku. Does it really need one? We can easily imagine what the mushroom looks like. We see it in our mind. Do you like mushrooms? Most people buy them in shops but there are still places in the world where people, young and old, go out and search for mushrooms to bring home to eat. Lithuania, for instance. Such fun! (Maybe it's not such fun for professional mushroom pickers though!) But you have to be careful. Some mushrooms are poisonous, as Issa warns us:

careful, children!
don't let those red mushrooms
bewitch you!

My favourite mushroom haiku by Issa was written in 1819:

from the treetop
the monkey points out
the mushrooms

In 1819, the Irish poet Riocard Bairéad died. Not many people know of him today. Two famous English-language writers were born in that year, John Ruskin in Britain and Walt Whitman in America.

What horses talk about

You should keep an eye out for haiku with adjectives and for those without. This next haiku has just one adjective—the word "misty"—and that's plenty.

misty day
horses chatting
in the field

You may have seen such a sight but even if you never did, you can imagine it. Horses are often seen standing close to one another. Talking about us, I'm sure. Issa wrote this horsey haiku in 1812. Check out what was happening in your country and in other parts of the world in that year, so long ago. Who was born or who died in that year? A Blasket-island poet, Seán Ó Duinnshléibhe was born in 1812. Find the Blasket Islands on a map.

The well-known classical composer Tchaikovsky wrote a musical work *1812 Overture* in that year. Let's see what else was happening: in January of that year, the poet Byron spoke in the British House of Lords and defended the people known as the Luddites.

Who were the Luddites? They were a group of men and women all opposed to the new-fangled machines and gadgetry that were part and parcel of the Industrial Revolution. These machines are going to take over, the Luddites thought. So, they went around wrecking machinery. Smash! Bang! Wallop!

Today, somebody who doesn't use modern technology is called a Luddite. I myself was once a Luddite. Not any more—though I confess I don't drive a car nor do I own a mobile phone, nor do I twitter. E-mail is fine but mobile phones disturb the bees! All those invisible signals criss-crossing their flight path. Quite a few of our buzzing friends never get back to the hive in one piece or if they do they have a headache that lasts a week, or more!

Modern Luddites call themselves Neo-Luddites. When paying a bill, Neo-Luddites insist on talking to a human being. They have no time for automated services and talking machines. Are they right?

In March, 1812, an earthquake destroyed Caracas, the capital of Venezuela. In June of that year, a war broke out between America and Britain. (Neither the Americans nor the British would learn about haiku for a considerable time to come. There would be far less fighting in the world if we had more haiku!)

In October, 1812, Napoleon and his army retreated from Moscow. In Christmas of that year the Grimm Brothers published the first volume of their *Fairy Tales*. There you have it—a quick overview of some of the things that were going on in parts of the world in the year 1812. What was happening in Africa? What was happening in Asia? In Japan, Issa was looking at horses in a field! And today, NOW, this very moment, we can read and enjoy his observations:

misty day
horses chatting
in the field

Issa could be a bit rude at times, as in the next haiku. Rude? Not really! Haiku is natural—it speaks of Nature, the nature of man and beast; it observes natural functions. Haiku is not a cosmetic exercise. It does not engage in prettification. The goose, the butterfly, the monkey, the horse, they are fine as they are. No need to dress them up! No need to gild the lily, as they say.

So, Issa may have been dozing or dreaming one evening when all of a sudden—

a horse farts!
I awake to see
fireflies flitting

That's so funny! But it's also quite serious. How so? Many of us spend our lives not fully awake. If haiku has a message, then that's it. Wake up! Wake up to the world. Teeming with life it is. And light! Anything can snap out of our dream (if we want to) and allow us to see the light—even a horse breaking wind. Tune in!

What is lovely about the fart haiku is the juxtaposition, that is to say the pairing of images or events. The two events are unrelated, yet somehow the haiku suggests that the force of the fart had an effect on the fireflies! And as Issa awakes, he blinks, as if wondering what he has just heard, what it is he sees. It's probably the best fart-haiku ever written. Could you write one that is as good? Or better? Try! But first you must wait for the moment!

Zen-haiku Master, J W Hackett, has a fart haiku:

puppy stops playing
and look around with wide-eyed
surprise—her first fart

Is it possible to write a haiku about pee? Yep, with some help from the horse, again:

little chestnuts
peed on by the horse ...
all shiny and new

Read haiku by old and modern masters and you will begin to see the world as it is, as it can be, all shiny and new. In the world of haiku, every day is a new day, full of possibilities, full of the old, full of the new.

Do you like horses? Then one more horsey haiku, specially for you:

Autumn evening—
from somewhere another horse
answers with a neigh

Issa gives us the second neigh. He doesn't mention the first one at all. Life goes on before and after the haiku moment. Issa brings us into his world of sights and sounds to hear that second neigh. One horse responding to another. Issa responding to what he has just heard. All of us responding to his response, all of us part of the great chain of being. How wonderful to be so alert to the world and to know that we are all linked to life in its infinite variety!

❀

Do you agree with this?

All of us are watchers—of television, of time clocks, of traffic on the freeway—but few are observers. Everyone is looking, not many are seeing.

—Peter M. Leschak,

Mr Fox goes bananas

Another fine day Issa went out for a stroll…. Hold on. What do we mean by 'fine day?' It was a day of heavy hail. Could you describe that as a fine day? In a way, every day is a good haiku day. Hot, cold, wet, windy, dark, bright. It doesn't matter. There's a haiku moment somewhere out there, just waiting to happen! Will you be there for it, in the NOW?

So, on another fine day, Issa took a stroll and lo and behold—wait until you hear (and see) what he saw:

a fox
driven demented
by hailstones

Poor old Fox! He might have been a young fox, unused to hailstones; he probably hadn't a clue what was going on. An older fox would have known. Ah, hailstones… yes, I know what you are. Hmmm, remember you well from last year. No need to fret. Let's see now. Find some shelter.

Issa felt for the fox, for the animal's confusion and pain. We use more than our eyes when we write haiku. We use other senses too. We listen and, of course, our feelings come into play,

19

our heart goes out. This is the best thing that could happen to us. Let your heart go out. You want to be loved, I am sure, don't you? Everyone does. To love is the best way to be loved.

Hailstones hammering down on a fox's head. Not something you see every day. But it's amazing what you see once you start writing haiku, or taking notes for haiku—seeds that grow into haiku at a later date.

a fox/driven demented/by hailstones

It's a funny old haiku isn't it? But it's also full of feeling. Issa feels for the fox. He feels for anything that gets a bit of a battering. And all of us get hurt now and then, in some physical, mental or emotional way. Feel for all things and you become part of all things. Stop feeling and you cut yourself off from the world; slowly but surely you'll become less alive, less caring, less human. Then it's easy to fall out with ourselves and with others.

When he was a little boy, Issa probably played in the long grass, pretending to be a fox! That was one of the many games played in his part of the world. Today, thousands of games exist on screen. But not so long ago, childhood games were very much part of the natural world, varying according to region and season, using natural materials as toys or creating imaginary worlds out of nothing.

children
in the pampas grass—
playing foxes!

Would you like to know the Japanese word for a fox? *Kitsune*! Three syllables. Say it: *Ki-tsu-ne.*

❀

Kigo is the word used to signify the season we are in. What *kigo* do we have in the first fox haiku above? Hailstones! Of course. A *kigo* for Winter. Make a list of Winter *kigo*, based on your own observations. There are a few obvious ones. When you have these written down, think of a few more that are not so obvious.

Want a really really strong Winter *kigo*? Wolf poo!

the mere sight
of wolf poo—
how terribly cold it is!

True or false: there are wolves in Portugal. Guess. Find out if you're answer is true. Can you think of place names which tell us that wolves once existed in the area? Clashavictory is in County Tipperary, Ireland. If you didn't know Irish you wouldn't see any connection with a wolf. The original Irish for this preposterously anglicized name was *Clais an Mhic Tíre*, Wolf's Hollow.

The curious case of the giggling pig

Humour varies from one country to the next and between one nationality and another. Here is a haiku that Issa composed in the year 1807. It's quite funny, don't you think?

Winter wind
the pig
giggling in her sleep

I've never seen or heard such a thing but we can be sure that Issa wasn't inventing it. Inventing things is not something that happens very often in haiku. A haikuist doesn't need to put his hand to his heart and swear what he says is true. We know it to be true. Haiku is about something that happens. A true *haijin* doesn't make things up.

What made the pig laugh? Maybe she heard a *hototogisu* calling out. A *hototogisu* is a small cuckoo found in Japan. Isn't it a lovely word? Pronounce it slowly:

Ho-to-to-gisu

Five syllables. There's another cuckoo that lives in the mountains in Japan. She has a nice name too—*kankodori*. Say it: *kan-ko-do-ri*. A four-syllable word. Issa loved the *kankodori*. He often heard it singing in the snowy mountains where he grew up:

don't leave
don't leave, dear friend
mountain cuckoo

Such tenderness! Do you think he had a soft heart? Not really—but better a soft heart than be hard-hearted. Or half-hearted. He had a real heart! A full heart. What are the things that gladden *your* heart? Whatever they are, treasure them. One of the things that gladdens my heart is haiku! The other is Irish harp music. Three haitches: Heart, Haiku, Harp.

Don't leave! But, of course, the cuckoo will leave. It must. That's life! If the cuckoo didn't leave, it wouldn't be a cuckoo. It would be a stone.

Speak to the earth

Notice that he refers to the *kankodori* as his "friend". Oh yes, no lie; she *was* his friend, one of many such friends among animals, birds, even fleas and beetles. Like St. Francis, he saw them all as brothers and sisters. (Saint Francis used to practice spiritual talks and sermons on the birds!) The Bible says, 'Speak to the Earth, and it shall teach thee.' *(Job*, 12:8) Solomon (the prophet Sulaiman) also spoke to birds and ants!

Issa observed the creatures of the Earth and spoke to them from one end of the year to the other. Spoke to them? Yes—for sure. He saw them as companions and talked to them. In many ways, he was inseparable from them. The highest form of haiku occurs when inseparability is realized. Later we will see a remarkable haiku about the heavy snows of his native district, Shinano. It's remarkable because it shows Issa as inseparable— even from snow!

❀

Song of the earth

Aren't we really lucky that all birds have their own songs, each its own unique music! Wouldn't it be awful if they all sounded exactly the same? What would we do without the cuckoo? For Wordsworth, the cuckoo was a mystery:

> *Thrice welcome, darling of the Spring!*
> *Even yet thou art to me*
> *No bird, but an invisible thing,*
> *A voice, a mystery …*

Issa never tired of the cukoo:

after tomorrow
and the next day
a cuckoo

Millions of people have never heard the cuckoo. Are you one of those? John Clare wrote beautifully about the cuckoo:
Cuck cuck! It cries and mocking boys
Cry 'Cuck! And then it stutters more…
Maybe there are no mocking boys left because they do not listen to the cuckoo anymore. Of course, there aren't many cuckoos left to listen to. In many parts of the world, it's an endangered species. Maybe the Luddites are right. If progress means the end of cuckoos, should we not slow down a bit and consider what progress really means? I know what Mr Progress would say to that: 'What? You must be cuckoo!'
I love the repetition in the next haiku:

a cuckoo sings
for me, for the mountains
for me, for the mountains

We can hear the echo! Is there a living creature that cannot hear it?

the cuckoo!
flies and beetles
listen carefully …

One of the oldest poems in English starts like this:

> *Sumer is icumen in*
> *Lhude sing cuccu!*

> 'Summer has come in,
> Loudly sing, Cuckoo!'

Not everybody is impressed with the cuckoo. John Bunyan wrote:

> *Thou booby, say'st thou nothing but cuckoo?*
> *The robin and the wren can thee outdo …*

❦

Issa probably composed the butterfly haiku in Summer; his encounter with the fox happened in Winter. The next haiku was composed in Autumn. We know this because Issa mentions it! It's the first word:

> Autumn wind—
> the wandering crow
> blows back and forth

Above, below, to the left of him, to the right—all earth and all the heavens are teeming with haiku. This is what happens when you begin to read and write haiku. The whole universe becomes alive—throbbing, squawking, neighing, singing, whistling. And the beautiful silence, before and after. A haiku that has *kokoro*, feeling, heart.

Here is another haiku about a crow. It was written in the year 1809:

a long day—
crow flies by
mouth wide open

There is something slightly eerie about those three lines. Could it have been a long, muggy, breathless kind of day when nothing bothers to chirp or squawk? The crow, with open mouth, seems to be silent, frozen in time.

Another fine crow haiku of his:

winter wind—
the afternoon crow
cannot find its nest

This, too, says something about Issa himself and about the wandering life of many *haijin*. Who does not love the comfort of home, the warmth of the familiar? But many *haijin* deliberately moved away from the comfort zone in order to know the world better and to know themselves, tuning into the waters and the wild.

Here comes the Kogarashi

Poor crow! The wind that day must have been very rough indeed if the crow couldn't find its nest. In Japanese, the Winter wind is known as the *kogarashi*. Some words give us the shivers. There's something harsh and dark about this word, isn't there? Say it: *ko-ga-rash-i*

Four syllables. It means " tree-witherer". Once again, look how deeply Issa feels for crows. The wind is so strong (in the first haiku) that the unfortunate crow is blown all over the place—like a scrap of paper in a gale. Worse again, in the second haiku the crow is completely lost! I hope this never happens to you! Stay at home and make sure not to go out when the *kogarashi* is blowing!

When Issa was still a young teenager, his father made him leave home in the countryside and go to live in the city. Issa was a troublesome and troubled teen. He and his stepmother didn't get on. The city Issa was sent to was Edo (known today as Tokyo). Issa felt like a poor lost crow! He tells us this in his diaries. A bird without a nest.

Issa was a farmer's son but he wasn't cut out for farm-work. A local poet first taught him all about poetry and haiku. Issa took to composing haiku almost straight away. He much preferred writing haiku to labouring in the rice-fields.

Back then, it was a tradition among *haijin* and others to travel around Japan, walking from place to place, to scenic areas as well as shrines and temples. They kept a journal as they walked and described the people, customs and places they came across on their travels. This type of writing is known as *haibun*, prose with a sprinkling of haiku. In those days, Japanese people loved to visit temples and monasteries or visit the graves of famous poets—the grave of haiku master Bashō near Lake Biwa, for example.

Issa was always travelling, working as a *spalpeen* or migratory worker, or teaching haiku to pay for his food and lodgings. Sometimes he met with other poets on the road. (*On the Road* is the name of a famous American novel and its author, Jack Kerouac, was also a *haijin!*) How many other poets did Issa meet on his travels? Six? Twenty? In fact, he noted down the names of 250 haiku poets who were writing in Japan at the time.

Once he was keen to meet a Buddhist monk named Sarai, but when he finally reached his destination he found out that Sarai had died a full fifteen years before that! (Communication wasn't instant then as it is in our time.) He asked the high priest if he could sleep in the temple overnight. He was refused. Issa had to continue on his weary way and as he left the village that night he was feeling quite low:

darkness, darkness
I step in a puddle
on this unknown path

Feeling a bit sorry for himself, no doubt. Is there anything worse than being left out alone in the darkness—far from home—not knowing which direction or path to take. And then, to crown it all, feeling your way in the gloom, you step into a cold pool of water.

Although Issa's childhood was very difficult, he returned home whenever he got the opportunity:

away from home
only a short while and look—
a fine young bamboo!

The first thing he notices on his return visit is new growth. See the welcome he gives it, the praise. This is Issa's way—to respond to all living things and welcome them into his life, even fleas and mites!

Notice that there is a short break at the end of the second line in this haiku. In Japanese, this break is known as the *kire-ji*. A three-syllable word. Say it! *Ki-re-ji*. The little pause makes us wonder what's going to come next. Look! (Pause) Oh, a fine young bamboo! I wasn't expecting that!

Don't expect anything

A haikuist doesn't expect anything. He doesn't know what's coming next. You could say he exists in a constant state of expecting nothing so that whatever comes is always a surprise—whether it's a lovely, shining, new bamboo that presents itself before his eyes or finding himself stepping, miserably, into a cold puddle on a moonless night!

Another young bamboo is mentioned here:

> just as the young bamboo
> straightens itself—
> thunder

The young bamboo had been bent over by heavy rain. Slowly but surely, it straightens itself up again. But then—the sky lights up. It thunders. More rain on the way.

Any creature that struggles with the ups and downs of life—be it animal, bird, plant or human being—Issa feels for them again and again. It's as if there is no end to his compassion. And, in truth, there isn't. How could here be? True compassion is selfless, endless, all-embracing.

Now, here is a haiku he wrote in 1815. Try and find out what was happening where you live and in the wide world during that year:

> lightning bolt!
> a glimpse of
> Zenko Temple

In life, we often get just a brief moment to see or hear something. We have that one instant, one chance, and it's gone again. But you can capture those moments through the power of haiku. And it gets easier over time. Now, don't go out for a stroll and tell yourself—"I have to capture a moment!" Haiku doesn't work like that. Try and capture the moment without trying. Just be aware. Responsive. What eventually happens is that the haiku moment comes to you and captures you—rather than the other way around. Read enough real, nature-centered haiku and you will acquire the knack. The lightning bolt will strike!

❋

Secret of the crows

Stay alert! I have a little trick that helps. I'll share that secret with you now. Shall I? Ok! Here goes. Every time I hear a crow squawking, a smile lights up my face, or I start laughing. Or I wink. Or I make some gesture such as a thumbs up. Something happens inside. Some form of acknowledgement. Why? Because Crow helps me to stay alert. Awake. Even if I am dreaming, or working, reading, writing, meditating—even when tired, or as idle as a piper's little finger—the sound of Crow squawking brings me back to real, raw life again. I shake myself awake or if it's really, totally unexpected, I'm struck by lightning!

"Why the crow?" I hear you ask. Simple. The earliest memory I have is of the sound of crows making a racket in the trees near our house in a place called Kilfinane, the highest little town in County Limerick, Ireland. Are the crows still there? I was a baby in the pram when Crow first spoke to me. I sometimes say that Crow is my first language.

I learned that trick about the crow from the 15th century Japanese poet, Ikkyu. One day he was meditating in a boat on

Lake Biwa, or maybe enjoying a little siesta. Next thing, out of the blue, *Caw!* You could say that the crow's squawk penetrated right through him! Thanks very much for that trick, Ikkyu. Much obliged! When I unexpectedly hear *CAW!* more often than not it affects me like a lightning bolt. He may be black as night but he always brightens up the day for me; that's for sure.

Something similar happened to the poet Gerard Manley Hopkins. In his case it was the thrush! As far as we know it only happened to Hopkins once, not something that occurred repeatedly over a lifetime:

> *Thrush's eggs look little low heavens, and thrush*
> *Through the echoing timber does so rinse and wring*
> *The ear, it strikes like lightning to hear him sing...*

The alertness must be there for the lightning to strike! Pick any local bird or beast for your own wake-me-up-call! How about a cow or a dog, or a cat? Any animal or bird that you hear from time to time (but not all the time). Would it have worked if Ikkyu had heard a cow mooing instead of a crow cawing? Certainly. It would have emptied his mind in a flash. *Moo* means 'Emptiness'!

The cormorant with nothing

Let's talk about another bird now, the cormorant or *an chailleach dhubh* "the black hag" as she's sometimes called in Irish. Another word for a cormorant in Irish is *treathlach*. And yet another word is *broigheall*. Words! Where do they come from? Cormorants, where do they come from? These birds are common enough in Ireland, especially in coastal areas. The same is true in Japan. There are about 500,000 cormorants in Western Europe altogether.

In Japan, some fishermen train the cormorant to catch fish. They put a ring around the cormorant's neck so that it can't swallow a catch. It's becoming a thing of the past now, enjoyed by tourists. But it was real enough in Issa's day. Imagine Issa as he observes the cormorant at work. Suddenly, another haiku comes to him:

my favourite cormorant of all
the one who comes to the surface—
beak empty!

Once again, see and feel Issa's great love for every living creature! Why the empty beak? Maybe that particular cormorant was too young and inexperienced yet to learn his trade correctly. Of maybe the opposite. Was it too old, too tired? Why exactly he came up empty-beaked we don't know. Maybe he was just unlucky. (Some cormorants have all the luck!)

He dived under the water again and again but every time he came up his beak was empty. Whatever was happening, the fisherman wasn't too happy with him, that's for sure. And yet Issa is fonder of this cormorant than he is of all the smart ones, standing there proudly looking at their catch.

There is a lesson here. Maybe more than one. Haiku speak to us on many different levels. Think for a minute about people who may not be as well-educated as we are. Or what about people who are not good at learning things, not so good at school or at sport. Then think of the cormorant. Issa likes the weakest one in the flock. The cormorant might have been a failure in the eyes of the fisherman, but not in Issa's eyes.

There is more than pity here. There is humour as well. Failure can be funny too, sometimes. Why should it be a disgrace?

What's wrong with failure? Everyone can't get to the top. (Not everybody wants to.)

> my favourite cormorant of all
> the one who surfaces
> beak empty!

There is pleasant humour here, full of kindness, not the harsh humour of the cruel crowd which we sometimes see, a heartless laughter that follows the 'failure' of others. In today's world, people have far too much respect for money and the trappings of wealth. The cormorant has absolutely nothing, zilch—but he is top cormorant as far as Issa is concerned. Nothing or nobody is a failure in Issa's eyes. And he is right. All of us are perfect, behind our various little flaws.

When Ikkyu heard that crow breaking the silence of Lake Biwa, the squawk must have cleaned out his brain—leaving it empty! We like to fill our minds with all sorts of stuff, some of it useful, much of it useless. Issa is telling us in the above haiku that emptiness should not be despised. Nobody allows rubbish or trash to accumulate in the home. It's the same with mental trash. Don't let it pile up. Haiku is a form of spring cleaning of the mind, actually:

> dew on the gate—
> sparrows licking it
> clean!

Here is another haiku on the subject of cormorants. Issa is watching cormorants diving into the water again and again, fishing for so long that they are getting weary. But the fishermen don't want to go home yet. More fish! Come on! More! More!

they give out to them
exhausted cormorants
dive once more

This haiku could serve as a banner or as a motto for those who try to put an end to all forms of exploitation, bullying and cruelty in this world, such as sweat-shop slavery and training teenagers to become soldiers.

Did you ever see cormorants standing on a rock? The way they spread their wings. A lovely sight. What are they doing? Since they spend so much time under water in search of fish, when they come up for a breather they like to stand on the rocks, drying their wings.

children imitating cormorants—
their antics more wonderful
than the cormorants themselves

Earlier we had children imitating foxes. Now cormorants. Are these games still being played? So many games have been lost. So many traditions. Thousands of them. In haiku we read about changes happening all the time. Animals, birds and all sorts of creepy-crawlies are constantly coming and going, appearing and disappearing in Issa's haiku. Indeed, his very name, his pen-name or *haigo*, means "a cup of tea" or "a bubble in a cup of tea". Say this word aloud: *hai-go*. Two syllables. *Haigo*. A pen-name. Invent a pen-name for yourself. Go on!

❀

A bubble that you see in a bowl of soup or a cup of tea—it never lasts too long, does it? There one second, gone the next. And this was Issa's attitude to life. Nothing in this world lasts very long. A day dawns and then it's evening. Seasons never last very long.

the beginning of Spring—
sparrows at the gate
their little faces

❀

Now look here now!

Those sparrows are as alive today as they were when Issa sketched them all those years ago. The tiny faces of sparrows. This is haiku, seeing into the life of things, seeing with the heart. Just one adjective—'little'; it's enough. Many people (at least, those who aren't birdwatchers) look at a bird and just see a vague outline, often not even sure what kind of bird it is: Issa sees their little faces! He is almost maternal—or paternal in a maternal way!

Issa did not invent this charming scene. He is a witness, purely and simple. A witness to something very special, and yet quite ordinary. His witnessing makes it special. And he teaches us how to become witnesses like him. We do not actually see

Issa as a witness in the haiku. He has vanished. We are left with the little faces of the sparrows.

Someone who loved haiku and wrote his first haiku in 1949, the year I was born, was Robert Spiess (1921-2002). Robert once said:

"In haiku, time is always the same—*now* and the place is always the same—*here*."

Issa's maternal/paternal voice is heard in another sparrow haiku:

watch out, sparrow,
move out of the way—
horse coming!

He was only about nine years of age when he wrote his first haiku, or so they say. Not having any new clothes, he couldn't attend a local festival with all the other children—there were about 100 houses in his village at the time—and Issa had to stay at home. No one to play with. And then he saw a small sparrow. Where were its parents? It, too, was all alone:

come and play!
little orphan sparrow
come play with me

❀

Have you learned a few words of Japanese by now? You have indeed! You know a dozen or so words of Japanese. What are they? *Haiku, Issa, Kigo, Hototogisu, Kankodori, Kire-ji, Haigo.*

That's only seven. Did you come across another few Japanese words? Yes you did. What is the name for a haiku master? *Haijin!* Two syllables. Say it. *Hai-jin.* That's just eight words. The Winter wind?—*Kogarishi.* Yes, that's it. You're doing well! Fox? *Kitsune!* A form of writing that combines prose and haiku? *Haibun.* And let's not forget *Kokoro,* which means feeling, heart. Time for another new word—*senryu.*

A senryu is a lighter form of haiku, one in which the human being plays a more obvious role than Nature does. Senryu can be quite funny:

fresh grass...
a posh woman
leaves the trace of her big bottom

She also left a senryu behind—about her behind! Three syllables, repeat them—*sen-ry-u.*

Issa takes note of everything that he sees, big and small. What about this for keenness of observation:

dragonfly—
faraway mountains reflected
in his eyes

Toriawase means 'taking and putting together'. Say it. It has five syllables: *to-ri-a-wa-se.*

We have the dragonfly's eyes and, in them, distant mountains. This combination can give great energy and space to haiku, things reflecting off each other, heaven and earth, the distant and the near. A fusion. The author (and the reader) become part of this energy, this fusion. Becoming one.

Another word for this combination, this fusion, is juxtaposition. Here is a striking example of the heavens come down to earth:

mountain village:
even in my soup—
Autumn moon

Let's looks at some more juxtaposition:

the cry of a deer—
red leaves fall
as tears

Issa knew tears. All his children died young and he himself died before the last child was born, the only child of his not to die young. No matter how much he suffered, he kept faith:

keep faith, keep faith
things are as they are—
dew falls

Things are as they are! That's worth thinking about. Things are as they are, not as we would like them to be, not as we imagine them to be. Things are as they are and—a lot of the time—things are perfect. Perfect as they are. There's an amusing Irish expression for that: *faoi mar a chacfadh an t-asal é*—"as the donkey would evacuate it"! Just right!

melting snow—
the village
overflowing with children

In a way, Issa himself was a big child!

I could eat it!
that snow that falls
so smoothly, so smoothly

it sticks to everything
like butter—
Spring snow

Bad weather affects all of us. We are happy when the sun is shining but we often scowl when the weather turns cold and wet:

wood pigeon
complaining—
Winter rain

Issa was probably inside in his hut when he heard the pigeon giving out. The pigeon's cry goes through him. It wouldn't if he were a callous, thick-skinned type of fellow but Issa just can't help responding to the world. That's his nature. He's in tune.

Notice how the haiku has no full stop at the end. Rain continues falling! And the pigeon continues to complain. A full stop would put an end to everything. A haiku keeps going.

Haiku don't have titles as most poems do. They don't need titles. And small letters suit them just fine at the beginning of every line. The haiku is modest. It doesn't like to draw too much attention to itself or puff itself up!

The crow that was bullied

It's not just people who are guilty of bullying, as we see in the next haiku. One afternoon Issa was watching a flock of geese feeding in the rice-field. Next thing you know, he notices some bullying going on:

the small crow
is snubbed
geese in the rice field

✻

Tune in, for pity's sake!

A little crow snubbed by geese; they tell him to be off. Get lost! They don't want him with them in the field. Maybe the crow got a few nasty pecks too, as well as being snubbed! Anyway, this kind of bullying happens far too often. Whether directly or indirectly, somebody is told to get lost—maybe because that person is different in some way. Issa didn't like that kind of behaviour. He has great sympathy for that poor wee crow, surrounded by big fat geese and being insulted by them! It's not the crow's fault that he's not a goose, is it?

Bullying is always wrong. Bullying on a large scale is called war. Sure! What else?

To war-mongers we should say, 'Pick somebody your own size!' Or better still, 'Stop warring! Tune into what is best in people and what is best in the world. Let's all tune into each other and stay tuned!'

Issa favours the crow in the above haiku. Elsewhere we see him in full sympathy with geese. (Not just geese, of course, it's me and you and everyone everywhere who ever left home):

wild geese!
were you young ones too
when you left home?

❀

The first butterfly

People write letters to the paper when they hear the sound of the first cuckoo of the year. We always like the "first thing" for some reason, no matter what first thing that may be: the first snowdrop, the first call of the cuckoo, your first kiss, the first day of Spring:

first butterfly
of the year
bursting with energy

Issa's haiku, they too are bursting with energy! If his haiku were any longer, they wouldn't have the same energy in them. Issa condenses his story into one short parcel of information. In the Irish language they say: *Bíonn blas ar an mbeagán*: "Little things tend to be tasty."

We write haiku using three lines but the way they are written in Japanese is using one long line which goes vertically down the page. They say that a haiku is as long as a breath. A poem in the space of one breath. Count the syllables in the (last) haiku as cited above. Sixteen syllables isn't it? Seventeen syllables is what is normal in the Japanese tradition, seventeen syllables divided up as follows—5-7-5. Count the Japanese syllables in the next haiku (cited below) and you will get seventeen syllables in total. (The 5-7-5 pattern isn't adhered to very much outside of Japan, by the way.)

snowman—
he too has no interest
in clearing the snow

降る雪を払ふ気もなきかがし哉
Furu yuki wo harau ki mo naki kagashi kana

Five syllables: *fu-ru-yu-ki-wo*
Seven syllables: *har-a-u ki mo na-ki*
Five syllables: *ka-ga-shi ka-na*

Issa says no one is interested in sweeping away the snow and, by the looks of it, the snowman isn't going to lend a hand either. All this in seventeen syllables. It's best not to have more than seventeen syllables in your haiku. When you get a chance, count the syllables in all of the haiku in this book. See if you can find some with more than seventeen syllables. Could they be edited down, could one get rid of a word here and there, a word like "the"? What is the average number of syllables in all of these haiku? That's a small project for you to do, especially if you like maths—count all the syllables of the haiku in this book and work out the average number.

Would you like to learn another Japanese word now? *Haijin.* Say it aloud. *Hai-jin.*

This new word has two syllables. What is a *hai-jin*? (If you were awake, you would have noticed that I actually gave you this world earlier on! Stay awake! Or find a crow to help you stay awake!)

A haijin is a haiku poet or a haiku master—someone who instructs other haiku poets in the art of haiku. Let's list a few haijin: Issa, Buson, Chiyo-ni, Bashō, Shiki, Santoka. That's six. Which one of them is a woman do you think? Can you guess? What other haijin did we mention earlier? Hackett. Kyoshi. Kerouac. See if you can find haiku by these fine haijin.

✾

Issa's haiku often make us smile. He also composed sad haiku. Some of them are so sad they would almost bring tears to your eyes:

the pony that was sold
looks behind him at his mother—
Autumn rain

This is a universal sadness, the sadness of parting. It is found in the animal world and in the human world—the child's first day at school, looking back uncertainly at its mother; it's the sadness of parting everywhere. It's one of the things that makes us what we are, human beings, not machines. It's a amazing how much the weather (the rain) and the season (Autumn) add to that beautiful haiku. Every season makes an appearance in haiku:

out of the fog
a cow—
moo, moo, moo

We often hear the question, "What does that mean?" Well, what is the meaning of that haiku? Maybe it doesn't have any particular meaning. What does "moo, moo, moo" mean? Believe it or not, the word "moo" in Japanese means "nothing"! Emptiness! (We mentioned this before. Do you remember?)

Here's another haiku written in 1815:

your rice-field
my rice-field
the same green

What does this mean? Take your own meaning out of it. Maybe it too has no meaning at all? Or maybe it has more than one meaning. Is he saying that we set up false boundaries? Between neighbours? Between nations? Karl Marx believed that private property should be abolished. What do you think? What are the arguments for and against this belief?

❁

Do you suffer from molluscophobia?

Issa looked out one day and saw a snail out there under the rain:

first Winter downpour
stay inside, snail
stay indoors with me

Issa invites the snail to come in out of the rain, to live with him in his ramshackle cabin. In a way, it's a signature haiku. We recognise Issa immediately, friend of the flea, friend of the baby sparrow, friend of the snail. You can be his friend too!

First Winter downpour! There is something very immediate about the word 'first'. It's not just any old downpour—it's the first Winter downpour, first of many. This immediacy cuts through all sorts of distractions: it cuts to the chase, as they say.

Why did he like snails? Doesn't everybody? Seemingly not. Some people are afraid of them. This unusual condition is called molluscophobia. I hope you don't suffer from it, do you? The world would be a poorer place if Issa had suffered from molluscophobia! If he had a fear of fleas, lice and other organisms—what kind of haiku would he have written? My guess is that he wouldn't have turned into a haijin at all. Not the haijin we know and love today. (I hope you don't have haikuphobia, do you? That would be awful!)

Back to the snails! I suppose he liked snails because they seem so relaxed. Issa had seen people rushing constantly here and there—in towns and big cities, Edo, Kyoto, Nagasaki, Osaka— buying and selling, talking, talking and talking. The snail, however, is never in a mad rush; he slithers around silently, every now and again putting out his horns.

with little effort
the snail rises
and falls asleep again

It's hard to know sometimes if a snail is asleep or awake:

little snail
awake or asleep—
the same

❀

One day, Issa tried to come to the aid of a fly. Unfortunately, his efforts didn't have much effect and the fly came to a sad end:

Winter fly
that I saved—
swiped by the cat

We associate monkeys with countries like Africa and India but they are also found in Japan:

a monkey riding
on his mother's back—
freezing night

Notice how simple the language is here. No complex words
and all the better for that. Some writers like to use jawbreakers!
Why? Well that's their business. They have no place in haiku.
Simple language will do to describe snails, flies and monkeys.

❀

Pick out the haiku you like best from this book and use them
for something. You could make a bookmark for example. Or,
you could hang a picture on the wall, a haiku poster. If you
search for the meaning of the word *haiga* you will find out that
it means a haiku that is illustrated with pictures/ artwork/
calligraphy/photographs. There are many different styles and
types of *haiga*—from traditional style to more modern digital
techniques. Wouldn't this haiku make a striking *haiga*:

mountain bogey-man
Autumn moon
along his sleeve

A bogey-man is another word for a "scarecrow". A big moon
in the sky. A scarecrow standing by himself on the mountain
somewhere. The moon lighting up his sleeve. There is
something magical in that haiku, isn't there? Can you feel a
silence there too? Listen to the silence in this next haiku:

Spring rain
a mouse licks
the bamboo leaf

The patter of rain drowning out the faint sound of the mouse as it licks the bamboo leaf, drowning out all other sounds, creating a musical silence, the silence that was there before the rain, the silence that will be there again when the rain has stopped. But silence never lasts too long. The next haiku is a noisy one:

Spring rain—
quack-quack of ducks
that weren't killed

We can hear the rain falling and we can hear the ducks too as they enjoy the rain. These ducks haven't been killed yet for food. They will probably be eaten later on—but for the moment, we can listen to their quacking. Quack-quack!

Good-for-nothing duck!

One day Issa spotted a wild duck and was surprised to see that it was sitting alone by the edge of a lake—all the other ducks had flown away:

good-for-nothing duck
have you no wife or family
waiting for you?

Issa speaking directly to the duck! Just like he addresses so many other creatures. What is the story with this duck? We don't know. It could be a bit of a loner, or an eccentric. There's always one! Another day, Issa returned home and a duck was looking at him as if to say: "Who the hell are you, lad—where did you come from, huh?"

> a duck in the yard
> she glares at me
> when I return home

It's as if the more Issa confronts the creatures he sees—as a fellow-creature—the more they confront him. That's the way he liked it. After all, birds and animals share quite a lot with us, fear, affection, boredom (especially if they are in zoos), curiosity, hunger. Do they have a sense of humour? What do you think?

❀

Often, very little happens in a haiku. A breeze blowing. Dew falling. If Issa waited until some major event happened, he wouldn't have written as many haiku as he did.

> wren going west
> mouse
> going east

Nothing much happening. Then again, who knows? Something's afoot. Something (however small) is happening all the time. Movement. Life. Flight. Walk. Some little thing is happening. It's a big world with billions upon billions of life forms living and breathing around us.

> wren
> looking here and there—
> have you lost something?

Another wren causes him more concern:

> wren
> beneath the downpour
> dripping wet

In Irish, there is a phrase *Is leor don dreoilin a nead*: "All the wren needs is its nest." In other words, its nest might be small, but it is not insignificant, in fact it suits the wren just fine. She wouldn't feel comfortable in a big nest, the nest of a stork, let's say. Or the heron's nest! No, she would be completely lost! Her nest suits her exactly the way it is. (*The Heron's Nest* is the name of a haiku magazine, by the way. Look it up!)

It is the same story with haiku. Three lines are enough. A half-dozen lines would be far too much. It wouldn't be a haiku at all. It would be something else—a *tanka* or a *waka* or something like that. So, a haiku that goes over seventeen syllables begins to wobble. It no longer has essential compactness and immediacy. It needs editing!

❀

The importance of frogs

Things which seem unimportant are important. This is what Issa is telling us in the next haiku. Or, to put it another way; there is nothing in this world that is without importance; every living thing has its own significance:

he sits himself down
with a flop—
frog

Issa loved frogs, even if some of them appeared to be angry, amused or disgusted—for some reason or other!

staring at me
with a grimace—
frog

A bit of a staring match going on, maybe. Like the duck. Remember a little while back when Issa returned to his hut and a duck was glaring at him?

a duck in the yard
she glares at me
when I return home

Issa's mother died when he was still a young boy. He didn't get on with his step-mother. He was eighteen when she moved in. He makes frequent mention of mothers in his haiku, the one about the pony that we read earlier, the one about the small monkey and this one, for example:

> beak open
> waiting for his mother—
> chick in the rain

A touching scene. Many things reminded Issa of his own mother:

> mother!
> every time I look at the ocean,
> yes, every time

How beautiful! The beauty of the ocean reminds him of his beautiful mother. (Every mother is beautiful in the eyes of a child.) The ocean seems to stretch forever. So is the love a mother has for her child. Waves, endlessly coming and going, reminding him, perhaps, of his sore loss, of the brevity of life, just as in Shakespeare, in Sonnet 60:

Like as the waves make towards the pebbled shore
So do our minutes hasten to their end …

Tune in to the real world

Maybe it was a good thing that his stepmother was hard on him and gave him the odd smack. Why do I say this? Since he had to avoid his stepmother to escape her tongue-lashings, Issa found company amongst the trees and flowers, amongst butterflies. "Go to the pine," haiku master Bashō used to say. "Go to the bamboo!"—and this is exactly what Issa did.

What did Bashō mean by—"Go to the pine"? What he meant is that we can forget about all our troubles, forget about ourselves. Our troubles are in the mind. Stop thinking about yourself all the time. Take a break from virtual reality and social media and tune into the grass, the trees, the wind. Spend time with the pine and the bamboo. Become a pine, become a bamboo. When this happens, there is no such thing as "inside" and "outside" anymore. Look how Issa becomes one with the snow:

<blockquote>
from my heart
falling—
the snows of Shinano
</blockquote>

People who are in love often feel like this. No "yours" and "mine" or "you" and "me" anymore; nothing but unity. Issa watches the snow falling outside in Shinano—(an ancient region of Japan that has been re-named today)—but it's as if snow is falling within also. The barrier between the inner and outer worlds dissolves and is no more. Some people draw back when they feel this is happening. We are afraid of losing ourselves. Haiku teaches us that there is nothing to fear.

Persimmons falling!

I wrote something once which unconsciously echoed the above haiku. I was visiting Rakushisha, just outside Kyoto, in Japan. It's the hut of a haiku master, Kyorai (1651–1704). Kyorai trained as a samurai but he gave up the life of a warrior and turned to haiku. He had some fine persimmon trees and a merchant came to view them. The merchant liked the fruit and promised to come back the following morning and purchase the lot. But that night a terrible storm raged and all night long Kyorai could hear the persimmons crashing to the ground, his harvest ruined. Viewing the battered persimmons the following morning he looked then at the bare branches and could see the mountain that was hidden before then! It was an enlightening experience for him.

This is the haiku I wrote:

> Rakushisha
> persimmons are falling—
> falling on my heart

❀

The story of the chickens

Now, we'll look at a piece of prose by Issa, a piece that includes haiku as part of the text:

> I went on a pilgrimage to Tokaiji in Fuse. I felt sorry
> for the chickens that were following me along the path

and so I bought them a handful of rice in a house that was opposite the temple gates. I scattered the rice amongst the violets and the dandelions. It wasn't long before the chickens were fighting amongst themselves about the rice. In between times, pigeons and sparrows silently came down out of the branches of the trees and swallowed the rice. When the chickens returned, the other birds flew back into the trees again, slightly earlier than they had hoped.

I've no doubt that they were hoping the chickens would continue fighting amongst themselves a little bit longer. The samurais, the farmers, the tradesmen, the merchants and all of the others; this is exactly how they live their lives.

scattering rice
a sin—
the chickens kicking one another

At first, Issa thought that he was doing some good by scattering rice amongst the chickens. Instead, he put them all fighting with one another and fighting is a sin, according to the Buddha. You shouldn't fight with yourself or with others. Conflict (including self-conflict) is to be avoided. (Not a bad idea that!)

We'll end the first section of this book with a short anthology of Issa's poetry, as divided out according to the season in which they were written. The *haijin* or haiku poet writes about five seasons—Spring, Summer, Autumn, Winter and New Year.

Part 2
Haiku's five seasons

Part 2
Haiku's five seasons

Spring

gentle Spring day—
a mountain monk peeping
through the hedge

(Year unknown)

The year has moved out of its period of hibernation. Spring renews everything. Life abounds once more. Even the monk, isolated from the world, way up on a cold mountain, is curious as to what's going on.

half of it
is snowflakes—
Spring rain

(Year unknown)

a gravestone
almost invisible
in Spring mist

(Year unknown)

Do you belong to a culture which gives importance to gravestones? In many countries, the dead are cremated so there is no gravestone to tend, no need for flowers. There are some lovely gravestones in Japan, such as the gravestone of the haiku master Kyorai, previously mentioned. It's very simple, only forty centimetres tall and only one word on it: Kyorai.

Issa asked in one of his haiku that a little cricket look after his gravestone!

Let's look at another Spring haiku:

my pine tree
is grateful too—
Spring rain

(1804)

Thinking of the other—in this case, a tree—this is the proper way to live, the only way to live. Much of the misery and conflict since time began has been caused by not thinking of the other.

Say "thanks" more often, and mean it

Give thanks and praise! So much thanks and praise can be found in the haiku of Issa. What a lesson he teaches us all! *Moladh is buíochas le Dia*, praise and thanks be to God—this was once a very common saying in Ireland. One hears it less and less today. A pity. Giving praise and giving thanks take one out of oneself and one's own concerns. In the novel *John Splendid* by Neil Munro, set in the Gaelic Highlands of Scotland, we read about a lovely ritual. Before sitting down to dinner, you went outside to see if anybody happened to be on the road who might be hungry; that person was invited in to share the meal. Now, that's civilization!

Once, in the year 1810, a strange illness struck Issa and he couldn't speak:

> how frustrating—
> even the wild geese
> call to one another!

What do you think was bothering him? If he didn't recover his voice, he wouldn't be able to chant the name of Amida (Buddha). In praise! Find out about chanting and its importance in the various traditions of the world. You might even like to learn how to chant. It's a wonderful way to use your voice. Listen to chants on YouTube from other cultures and find out which ones appeal to your ear—and heart. African? Christian? Hawaiian? Buddhist? Jewish? Muslim? Vedic? Baha'i? You might be enchanted! Find out if chanting is or was a part of your culture. Have you ever heard *cante jondo,* the deep chant of the Gypsies? If not, give yourself a treat and find it now on YouTube.

Why not download an MP3 of a Pure Land chant and tune into the type of sound that Issa would have known. He was tuned into ducks as well!

> Spring rain—
> ducks come flip-flopping
> up to the gate

That was in 1805. We can still hear them, still see those same ducks today.

thieving crow!
cloaked
in Spring mist

(1805)

Thinks he can hide, does he? Hah, you can't hide from Issa. Not that the crow need fear him. Issa obeys the commandment of *ahimsa*, non-violence. Many great men and women have followed this path, St Francis, Gandhi, Martin Luther King, Nelson Mandela, Aung San Suu Kyi. What do you know about these people?

By the way, you don't have to be a grown-up to work for peace. Samantha Smith, a girl from Maine, USA, was only ten years of age when she wrote a letter to the leader of the Soviet Union during the Cold War. Read about her short but eventful life.

Pickles for sale!

Spring rain—
on the ancient road
a seller of pickles

(1806)

What are pickles? Do you know how they are made? It's not so difficult to make pickles. Pick something and pickle it— maybe a cucumber? The English word *pickle* comes from the

Dutch word *pekel*, meaning brine. That gives us a clue as to how food is sometimes preserved—in salt water.

Notice the contrast in the pickle haiku. Spring. The world begins to blossom anew, and Issa encounters a pickle seller on an ancient road. Pickles that preserve. New fresh growth of Spring contrasting with preserved pickles. Ancient road. It's all new roads today, isn't it? Sometimes the heart longs for ancient roads!

Is there a period of ancient history that attracts you? What about recent history? What do you know about your great-grandmother, for instance? What was her name? Your great-grandfather? Tune into your own people, into all people. Tune into yourself.

Have you ever heard of Shinto? It's a way of honouring the earth and honouring our ancestors. Next time you look at a mountain, a river or a waterfall, remember—your ancestors may have stood and gazed at the very same view. Or perhaps your ancestors came from a distant land? (Come to think of it, we have all come from somewhere else!)

❀

Summer

heat haze—
a dog scurries after
a field mouse

(Year unknown)

The rising sun

We've had Spring mists and now Summer heat hazes but it doesn't matter, Issa's penetrating glance is always there, to view the world clearly, with amusement, with compassion, with sorrow, resignation, or with joy.

Summer mountains
all being washed (you'd think!)
by the rising sun

(1800)

The sun is rising and already Issa is composing haiku. It must have come very natural to him. *If Poetry comes not as naturally as the leaves to a tree it had better not come at all*, as Keats said.

By the way, what do the Japanese call their country? Japan? No. They call it Nippon, officially, or Nihon, casually. And what do these words mean? The Land of the Rising Sun.

short Summer night
frogs are croaking—
complete nonsense

(1813)

Can you picture Issa listening intently to the frogs? Could he be in bed? Are the frogs keeping him awake? Anyway, he doesn't think much of their drivel. Hold on! Actually, he adored frogs. Who doesn't! Maybe he liked their nonsense too. Why not? There's a lot to be said for nonsense.

Many years later, another such night. This time it's not frogs:

short Summer night—
the sport of turtles
in the field

(1825)

Did he envy the turtles, I wonder? After all, this is the year 1825 and Issa is not as mobile as he used to be. He only has two more years on this earth. No, I don't sense any envy there. If anything, he shares in their play. Whatever about the body, his mind is still as playful as ever. This sharing in the life of all things on earth is the mark of a great haiku master.

❀

Autumn

looking at the mountain
looking at the sea …
Autumn evening

(1790s)

Things as they are, just as they are. No more.

the pine tree that I planted
it too grows old—
Autumn twilight

(1803)

All is change, all is flux, Issa reminds us. Everything has its phases. A year later:

looking at my wrinkled hands—
night time
Autumn rain

(1804)

Look at your own hands. Are they wrinkled? No? Any wrinkles on your face? Well, if not, given time wrinkles will appear, as on a leaf. Accept them. Issa reflects on his wrinkled hands. It is Autumn. A time of decay. But he is not fighting the wrinkles. You might as well fight the rain, the snow, Time itself. Acceptance. We find so much acceptance in the haiku of Kobayashi Issa.

snail
what job have you got?
Autumn twilight

(1808)

That's very Issa, isn't it? Talking to a snail. And, indeed, if you watch the slow progress of a snail, you might well ask, what is he up to? Where is he going? What is he doing? Has he no timetable, no schedule, no duties, no office to go to?

autumn wind whistles
through what's left
of my teeth

(1808)

We like to show ourselves off in the best light but Issa isn't vain. His teeth are going? OK, his teeth are going, he's not going to disguise the fact. The Irish singer Shane MacGowan had such bad teeth that a record company decided to airbrush them. The singer was not too happy at the time with what he saw as a distortion.

scarecrow—
he doesn't know what he is:
Autumn evening

(1811)

Ah! This is quite amazing. Of the tens of thousands of haiku I have read, this is one of the strangest. No, of course he doesn't know what he is, poor scarecrow. Sometimes it's the same with ourselves. We don't know who we are. Or we think we are such-and-such when, really, that is not who or what we are at all. At heart. We identify with our name, our gender, our country, our language, our politics, our religion, our opinions … A thousand things.

Haiku brings clarity to this question—and to many others. The clarity of being a witness. A witness of fleas, of shadows:

they're back
those fleas I got rid of …
Autumn rain

(1813)

Autumn wind-
shadow of the mountain
trembling

(1814)

67

❀

Winter

little mice—
don't piddle
on my old Winter quilt!

(Year unknown)

You would be angry, I'm sure, if someone piddled on your bed-clothes, wouldn't you? But you wouldn't give out to a two-year old toddler. Similarly, Issa isn't angry with the mice. He's just giving them a gentle warning.

Issa does not have to go to the ends of the earth to find haiku. Haiku find him. Haiku are happening all around him, all of the time. They are happening all around you, as well, morning, noon and night. Tune in! That's all you have to do.

tree stump-
mushrooms huddled together—
Winter rain

(1806)

It's a while since we tuned into syllables. Let's count the syllables again in the original:

切株の茸かたまる時雨哉
kirikabu no kinoko katamaru shigure kana

When you are tuned into haiku, see what happens:

> first Winter shower—
> the world fills up
> with haiku
>
> (1810)

Yes. As Ummon says, *Every day is a good day*. For the haikuist, there is always something happening, or not happening, or about to happen:

> Winter trees—
> ancient sound
> from long ago
>
> (1811)

Haiku is about tuning into the present. The present sounds like it might be new all the time but, of course, it is also old. How old is the wind? How old is light? How old are you? We are ancient and we are new, as is the world.

The fifth season

And that's our cue for the last haiku season, the New Year:

> New Year's Day—
> nothing new
> my hut's in a mess

Part 3
Kigo: keys to the seasons

Part 3
Kigo: keys to the seasons

It frequently happens in Japanese haiku that a season isn't actually mentioned at all; instead, a strong (or subtle) hint is given. A *saijik*i is a special dictionary or list of words that provides us with *kigo*—that is, words or images that relate to different seasons. Say this word aloud: *sai-ji-ki*

Let's look at some *kigo* now, beginning with *kigo* that relate to Spring. Snow melting? Obvious enough. Can you think of a few others? Make a list, based on your own observations. The sowing of plants and seeds, for instance:

> rainy day
> alone,
> diligently planting rice
>
> (*Year unknown*)

Whatever the weather, it was vital to plant rice on time. What other types of work do we associate with Spring? Ploughing. Life was tough in Issa's days, wasn't it? Rain falling. Issa out in the fields planting rice. Another haiku has hailstones lashing down on the plougher. But, look—swallows!

a good day
to plough the rice field
swallows have returned

(1822)

How he loved swallows, loved their bird-talk, the way they call and sing to one another:

they all
have plenty to say—
swallows

(1824)

Indeed they do—and they have just announced that it's time for a break. 1824, the year of the above haiku. What was going on in the world? Lots. Simón Bolívar came to power in Peru, in January of that year. In May people heard Beethoven's *Symphony Number 9* for the first time ever in Vienna. That same year Archbishop Thomas Croke is born, the person after whom Croke Park, in Dublin, was named. Two months earlier, in March, 1824, the Anglo-Irish poet William Allingham was born. Here is the first stanza from one of his best-known creations:

Up the airy mountain,
  Down the rushy glen,
We daren't go a-hunting
  For fear of little men;
Wee folk, good folk,
  Trooping all together;
Green jacket, red cap,
  And grey cock's feather!

Very different from haiku! I learned that poem at school except that instead of "grey cock's feather", I remember the words "white owl's feather". Which of the two versions is the original or correct one—who knows? Anyway, it's a charming poem. (I have to admit, though, that I much prefer Issa to Allingham and his ilk.)

Where were we again? (Those wee little men with their red caps have led me astray!) Oh, yes, we were with Issa, listening to swallows. Another bird that Issa was particularly fond of and which often stands for Spring is the skylark.

> lily in bloom!
> and the lark
> singing her heart out
>
> (1810)

You could almost imagine the lark was singing in praise of the blooming lily. This interconnectedness is part of the power of haiku. Who knows why the lark was singing? For the same reason that Issa was composing haiku. That's what they do. That's what they do best!

Another Spring *kigo* is the nightingale:

> when the nightingale
> goes into the pine—
> the voice of the pine
>
> (1803)

The singing bird went out of sight and disappeared into the trees—but still kept singing. Issa heard the tree, singing! This often happens in haiku—one element or image merging with another. The reader merges too. For a second, we become the pine, the voice of the pine.

Another *kigo* that describes Spring is the cherry blossom, *sakura,* the best-known *kigo* of them all:

>although my rice sack
>is empty—
>cherry blossoms

Issa has run out rice. The sack might be empty but his heart is full, full of the joys of cherry blossoms. You can't eat them but they are so beautiful that he forgets—for a short while, at least—about the lack of rice.

Sakura is the Japanese word for cherry blossoms. (I once stayed in a small hotel in Tokyo for a couple of nights, the smallest hotel in the city—and that was the name of the hotel. *Sakura.*) Say it aloud: *Sa-ku-ra*

In the next haiku, Issa apologizes to the *sakura,* worried that smoke from his pipe might pollute them!

>cherry blossoms—
>please excuse
>my pipe

>(1816)

Snakes alive!

Now we come to the subject of the snake. To which season does the snake belong? Any idea? It depends, I suppose! If the snake is going into its home, that's a Winter *kigo*. A snake emerging from its home? Spring *kigo!*

Summer now. Can you think of any *kigo* that might relate to Summer? Make a list, based on things you hear, or see, or smell! Images of heat and sun come to mind. And perspiration.

One of the animals often associated with Summer in Japanese haiku is the baby deer or fawn:

> don't teach the fawn
> your tricks
> noisy crows!
>
> (*Year unknown*)

Issa suspects that the crows are up to some sort of devilment. He doesn't want the fawn to learn any bad tricks from them. The mosquito is associated with Summer too.:

> night after night
> absolutely tormented by them—
> fleas, mosquitoes
>
> (1801)

It's not usual for Issa to be giving out about fleas and mosquitoes. This haiku must refer to someone else! We need to find shade from the heat of the Summer sun:

leafy shade
of the melon tree as his pillow—
kitten

(*Year unknown*)

Another Summer *kigo* is the snail:

little snail
look! look
at your shadow

(1814)

Autumn *kigo*? Any ideas? The colour of the leaves changing would be an obvious one. Leaves falling from the trees:

red leaves
blowing against him…
scarecrow

(1805)

You could paint a lovely picture of that scene—and many other scenes throughout this book! What do we call a haiku that has a picture accompanying it? *Haiga.*
This haiku was written ten years later:

stuck
to the young fawn's bum—
red leaves

(1815)

Make a list of Autumn kigo from what your senses tell you. The Milky Way is an Autumn *kigo* because it's easier to see it in Autumn than during any other season of the year—in Japan anyway. Find out what the Milky Way is called in other languages. Heaven's River (*ama no kawa*) is what it's called in Japan. Say those words aloud: *a-ma no ka-wa*

In Latvia and Estonia, people call the Milky Way the Path of the Birds. In Thailand they refer to it as the Way of the White Elephant. Which name do you like best? Check out the legend of the Milky Way on the Isle of Man.

Haiku are written not only about things that we see and feel and smell and touch around us but also about what we hear. Thunder, for example. Thunder is an Autumn *kigo*:

**mixed in
with thunder-
the call of the pheasant**

(1804)

That is a delicate example of something mentioned a little earlier; one thing merging with another, one element running into another, or echoing it in an unusual way. You could say that an early form of haiku was the opening stanza of a *renku*, linked verse composed by a group of poets at a party. The opening stanza had 5–7–5 (17) syllables and the link, or response, had 7–7 (14). Next link had 5–7–5 again and so on in a chain of verse. It's as if the haiku, today, still retains something of the notion of that original echo or response.

Tuning into *mushi*

What are *mushi* do you think? Guess! Any idea? No? *Mushi* are small insects that sing in the Autumn. Grasshoppers. Crickets. Issa tuned into them a lot! To get a present of singing crickets in a cage is not uncommon in Japan. Children play with insects and even breed them—the rhinocerous beetle known as *kabutomushi*, for instance, and the stag beetle known as *kuwagatamushi*.

among the insects
not even one old voice
to be heard

(1817)

Insect music gave Issa great pleasure. He would listen to them and conduct the insect choir with a paper fan!

a deer calls
and the insects
are not asleep either

(1820)

You came across the *kakashi* previously, didn't you? What is it again? The scarecrow! The poser who stands out in the field! The *kakashi* is an Autumn *kigo*.

night fall—
me and the scarecrow
just the two of us
(1818)

What effect does this haiku have on you? Is it scary? Weird? A feeling of loneliness? Or a feeling of companionship? Do you remember one of the scarecrow haiku we had previously:

red leaves
blowing against him...
scarecrow

That was from 1805. The 1818 haiku above, is it the same scarecrow I wonder?

Another Autumn *kigo* is dew:

morning dew-
more than enough
to wash my face

(1820)

Mushrooms are gathered in Autumn. You can see from the next haiku that Issa got some help with his mushroom-gathering:

from the top of the tree
a monkey points out
the mushrooms

(1819)

Where you find trees you find woodpeckers! The woodpecker is an Autumn kigo. He doesn't go tap-tap-tap just for
the fun of it. He is boring a hole in a tree! Once he has the hole
made, he reaches in with tongue, catches insects that are inside
the tree and eats them for his dinner. One day Issa came across
a woodpecker and look what he was doing:

the woodpecker
tapping the tree-trunk—
practice!

(1819)

Wintry days, wintry nights

The changing colour of leaves is an Autumn *kigo;* a Winter
one is the sight of leaves on the ground:

the wind
brought enough fuel for the fire—
fallen leaves

(1815)

Issa lived in a mountainous area in Japan known as Shinano. It used to be quite cold there in Winter. Occasionally, we hear Issa complaining about the weather but most of the time he just puts up with it.

in my cabin
cold nights, cold days—
ah well

(*Year unknown*)

Sake is a wine made out rice—a rice-wine. It's a drink that can be heated up before taken, if desired. Issa often ran out of sake even when he could have done with a drop to warm himself up.

run out of sake
that's life—
cold night

(1793)

If it was cold inside, it was even colder outside and uninvited visitors often came to stay in Issa's house:

the mouse
slips in furtively—
cold night

(1811)

The little mouse is in search of food and warmth. It often happened that Issa himself had no food left, especially in Winter:

isn't it a poor dinner
in the palm of my hand—
sleet

(1803)

Issa was 53 years of age when he wrote the next haiku. He must have been absolutely frozen with the cold:

I feel
my knees have aged—
cold night in the hills

(1813)

They say that it was in the Blackstairs Mountains in County Carlow that the last wolf in Ireland was killed. That was in 1786. In 1818 Issa composed this:

wolf's poo—
how cold the grass
is!

Yes, the sight of that would make you feel cold, alright. (Do you remember the previous wolf-poo haiku?)

It's cold, too, in the next haiku, although there is the hint of warmth:

> young deer
> licking one another—
> frosty morning

(1819)

From a tender scene to a slightly bizarre one:

> a snowball-
> the horse
> ate it!

(1813)

Just like that!
We meet some old friends of Issa—sparrows—in this next haiku:

> sparrows gather
> and emit cries of praise...
> snow Buddha

(1815)

Where there is snow you will find snowmen. Somebody has made a snow Buddha—maybe the poet himself? Issa imagines that sparrows are chanting in praise of the Buddha. His own kindly nature and his Buddhist ideals, combine them and you have his intense interest in all living things of every shape and size:

> snowy day—
> now and then
> the fly goes out to play
>
> (1823)

Finally, the New Year:

> not even a shred
> of pine decoration...
> the year's first dawn
>
> (1804)

Everbody else's house has pine and bamboo decorations for the New Year. Issa's hut is like his haiku—unadorned, simple, honest and unpretentious, like his own heart.

There we leave the world of Issa, but surely not for ever. You'll tune in again, won't you, to a world of flitting butterflies, foxes driven mad by hailstones, geese on their tippy-toes, monkeys, deer, fleas, giggling pigs, mushrooms, farting horses, flitting fireflies, snails, cuckoos, scarecrows, sparrows, cormorants, wrens, frogs, swallows, mice, snakes, singing insects. What a world!

Part 4
My haiku and I

Part 4
My haiku and I

*M*y haiku and *I*? I like to keep 'my', 'I' 'me' and 'mine' out of 'my' haiku. Here's one I wrote to remind me of that fact. We had a pond, once, in the back garden. It had tadpoles:

> a heron has just gobbled up
> all of my tadpoles—
> my! my! my! my!

My, oh my! They weren't *my* tadpoles, were they? Of course not. There is too much emphasis on ownership in this world of ours. (Of *ours*?!) Possessions! Nobody owns the air, the wind, the moon, the sun—though somebody might some day, unless we're careful!

> flowers in a vase—
> a cat walks
> through a bare garden

When I am asked to explain some haiku of 'mine', I usually say: 'I don't have any definite explanation for that.' What does a rose mean? What does the moon mean?

I wasn't the person who created the image in the first place. It created itself. It just happened. The haiku was written because I happened to be there at the time. Aware. Conscious. Tuned in. That's all. When I first observed this scene, I had a choice. I could have simply ignored the scene, my thoughts elsewhere; or, the scene could have been partially registered and then quickly forgotten.

What happened was that I saw the vase and—beyond it, outside—a cat prowling a bare garden. This is the double-vision, so to speak, of haiku, one thing answering another, merging into each other in clarity. Seeing with the eyes. And seeing with the heart. One thing leading to another and to the birth of a haiku. Nothing quite like that ever happened to me before or since. Every birth of a moment is unique. And so, haiku registers unique moments, unique insights, insights into nothing really and yet … life would be dull, mechanical and meaningless without these 'meaningless' moments. Now do you know the 'meaning' of the above haiku?

It must be over thirty years ago now since I wrote that haiku. Those flowers withered a long time ago. The poor cat is dead too. But those same flowers remain fresh and the cat is still walking through the bare field the same way she did all those years ago. Haiku always happens now. It belongs to now—the present—even if there are elements of the past and the future in it as well.

I have other cat haiku. Am I fond of cats? Not particularly. But you can't ignore them, can you? Slinky creatures:

> a glimpse of a god
> in the eyes of a cat
> following a moth

Now, what does that mean! We always seek a meaning or an answer for everything, don't we? A woman from Kerry was once asked:

"Is it true that a Kerry person always answers a question with another question?"

And the answer:

"Who told you that?"

We often ask or we are asked: WHAT DOES THIS MEAN? We are constantly looking for answers and cramming our heads with them. This isn't true in every part of the world, however. For example, the renowned Korean poet Ko Un: he thought he was so clever that he knew everything! Needless to say, he didn't. Far from it! "MOO!" his Master said to him one day. ('Moo' means emptiness or void; "nothing". Remember Issa's favourite cormorant? The one who came up with nothing!)

"Think about that for a while Mr Smarty Pants!" Ko Un's teacher said. "Your head is too full of thoughts. *Moo* will help you empty yourself upstairs and clear out your overload!" And, guess what? It did. It helped him a great deal; in fact. Ko Un wrote more than 150 books and is still writing today. He found freedom in the void, in the emptiness. He found space, a wonderful never-ending space, stretching back, stretching sideways, stretching forward, expanding in all directions, space in which to spread his artistic wings and fly in whatever direction the winds blew him.

My next cat haiku brought me to outer space!

from what unknowable universe
beyond Hubble—
the cat's green stare

Yes, I tried to outstare a cat once. It was freaky. Those green eyes. And nothing was said. Everything was unspoken. It was a *Moo* moment rather than a *Mee-ow* moment! But it was a moment. An encounter. A close encounter. In a way, it was not unlike Issa's close encounter with a wild goose at the very beginning of this book. It can only happen in silence. It's an above-and-below-moment, too, this world and some other world.

Lovers can lose themselves in a glance! They become so tuned into each other that they are momentarily One. And so it is with haiku. Doho, a disciple of Bashō, the most renowned of all haiku masters, explained his master's teaching by saying that description of the object is not enough. One must enter the object:

"Learn about the pine from the pine and the bamboo from the bamboo—the poet should detach his mind from self … and enter into the object … so the poem forms itself when poet and object become one."

Lovers need not say a word. The loving glance, the loving gaze works perfectly in silence. In haiku, too, we must see with the heart or we are not seeing at all, a heart robed in silence.

Eugen Gomringer showed us silence in a concrete poem from 1954:

silencio silencio silencio
silencio silencio silencio
silencio   silencio
silencio silencio silencio
silencio silencio silencio

There is a void, emptiness, stillness within haiku poetry. Haiku is not something that is constrained within a box— something that is defined or comes to an end with a full stop. There's a void in haiku and it's up to the reader to fill in that void, or simply enter it. In that void, thoughts get washed away. Don't panic! They'll be back.

Sometimes, when people show me a haiku they have written, I say to them—'Too full. Where is the emptiness? It's a clutter. You have put too much into it!' A cat walks through a *bare* field. Free and easy. This cat wouldn't be free if there were other things in the field getting in her way—rocks, flowers, weeds—and so on. There's something bare or pared-down about haiku. Tell the bare truth, they say. Make the truth bare. Plain and simple.

Another cat haiku:

frosty morning ...
a dead cat's paw
reaching to the sun

See it? See the above-and-below-nature of it? Tune into *zoka*! *Zoka* is the magic of the seasons, the creative force in Nature. Tune in, whatever the weather: tune into frost, into sunshowers, heat hazes, autumnal fog. *Zoka*!

A haiku doesn't need much in the way of ornamentation. Simple and bare. I loved that bareness from the very first moment I began to read haiku. The first book about haiku that I read was one by an Englishman who lived in Japan, R. H. Blyth. It was Blyth who set me on the haiku road. Here's something he said:

The sun shines, snow falls, mountains rise and valleys sink, night deepens and pales into day, but it is only very seldom that we attend to such things... .When we are grasping the inexpressible meaning of these things, this is life, this is living. To do this twenty-four hours a day is the Way of Haiku. It is having life more abundantly.

Haiku, Volume 1, p. 11.

How true. Rarely do we attend to such things. It would be a different world if we were more attentive, to the world, to others, to ourselves. There was a man who lived in Greece long ago. (Actually, we've mentioned him earlier!) Heraclitus. He said people were asleep! This is where haiku comes in. A person who composes haiku, he/she is not asleep but, rather, awake to the world!

foghorn at dusk—
little by little
the world disappears

Haiku relate to things that we see, hear, feel, touch and smell. The world unveils itself through haiku but sometimes it conceals itself too. I live in a place called Glenageary, in County Dublin. This town is very near Dún Laoghaire where the ferry crosses the sea between Ireland and England. When it was foggy, you could hear the sound of the foghorn coming from the ferry-port. Slowly but surely, as the fog thickens, the world disappears.

Haiku reflect the impermanence of the world we live in— sometimes directly, sometimes indirectly. Nothing in this world lasts. In fact, the foghorn that I recorded above will never sound again. New technology has replaced it. It's gone. Redundant.

sheep droppings
eight … ten … a dozen
all the same

What can we say about that haiku? Nothing in creation is more important than the next thing. The swan is no more important or beautiful than a crow is, for example; a mountain isn't more important than a sheep's droppings. And even if the sheep's droppings are all alike, that doesn't lessen my respect for them as singular elements of the natural world.

Haiku is a very democratic form of poetry. The rose is no more beautiful than the dandelion. The person who composes haiku does not think too much about it; you don't have to judge, or make up your mind about things, just stay open, in tune. That's all. Simple really. But we can have immense difficulty with the simplest things. Strange, isn't it?

All you need to do is to step back for a moment, allow space to witness and enjoy the show that the world is staging all the time! Marvel at it! Your response doesn't have to be clever or even original. Let it be simple and sincere. Learn from Issa.

OK. Let me take you on a haiku trip! Because that's what I do. When I go somewhere, I usually feel like writing *rensaku*, that is a sequence of haiku about a certain place at a certain time of the year.

First stop, Achill Island, Co Mayo, Ireland:

Achill Island
oyster-catchers
stare at visitors

Tourists are often curious about things and go around gawping at everything, cameras flashing. In this haiku, however, things have been turned right around. It's the oyster-catchers that are staring at the visitors!

The Irish lexicographer Dinneen had this to say about the etymology of the Irish word *roilleach* (oyster-catcher), a bird that has a central place in the folklore of County Mayo:

> The oyster-catcher or sea-pie, a bird that haunts the shore, has red bill and legs and has its coat variegated like the magpie; the *roilleach* was web-footed originally as the *faoileán* [seagull] is now. The *faoileán* asked for the loan of the *roilleach's* swimming gear and refusing to return the web-feet has worn them ever since, *iasacht an tsnáimh thug an roilleach don fhaoileán an iasacht nach bhfuaireas ariamh ar ais is nach bhfaighidh go deo,* the loan of the swimming gear which the sea-pie gave the seagull, a loan that never has been and never will be paid...

Let's set sail now for Kerala in Southern India. Find it on the map.

> heat shimmers—
> an old cyclist
> rides into infinity

Heat shimmers. Did we come across this motif before? Yes we did! Issa witnessed them as well!

This one is from Mumbai, formerly known as Bombay:

> Mumbai
> rags on a pavement
> a body stirs in them

Let's go from heat to snow. The month is April and I am in the Catalonian Pyrenees. Find them on the map.

with each call
the cuckoo
melts the snow

somewhere in the fog
a little bell
around the horse's neck

Back to India again, this time in Bangaram, part of the Lakshadweep Islands. It might take you a little longer to find them on the map! Are they east or west of the great sub-continent?

even the butterfly
takes a rest
on a hammock

So far I seem to have a lot in common with Issa: cuckoos, horses, butterflies. I don't think he had a cyclist though, did he? No, I'm sure he never saw one or even heard of one. He saw turtles of course:

a glimpse of a turtle
his eyes:
and what they have seen

Well, what did the turtle see? Things that you and I never saw and never will, perhaps. Make a list of things which that turtle may have seen!
I wrote a *rensaku* once called *Empty Moors*. Any guesses where I might have been? Not far from Ireland, as it happens. The Scottish Highlands:

bare moor
not even
a hare

That's bare, to be sure. I visited a fishing village with a lovely name Ulapul (in Gaelic), Ullappol (in English):

a rusty boat
stole its colour
from the moor

Travelling south now, to North Wales in the depth of winter:

a cow looks over
Caernarfon Bay
without knowing why

a low sun
shadows flee
across battlefields

suddenly
the universe expands—
wild geese honking

Does travel broaden the mind? Haiku does. Literally. I felt the whole sky above me, the universe (and me with it!) expanding. Another above-and-below experience. Notice that I put a hyphen between these words. Why? Because they are connected. I'm not talking about ABOVE and BELOW. I'm saying above-and-below. Connected. As One. This is called *Advaita* or Non-Duality.

Haiku can be a connecting device in which we see all things as One. It doesn't happen all the time and, frankly, if all haiku were the same above-below experience all the time, we could tire of it. But it's hard to get away from. Father Thomas Hand, S.J. spent 29 years in Japan and wrote haiku under the name Hando. Here is an example of one of his above-below experiences:

the puddles on the pavement
carry the moon, the stars
and cherry blossoms

Could *you* have an experience like that? Of course! Why not? It's quite an ordinary experience, really, but the feel of it can be quite extraordinary. This book is about sharing such feelings with you. Puddles on the pavement. Time to tune into puddles!

Sure, we're not always in the mood. Remember Issa stepping into a cold puddle on a dark night? But in Hando's puddles we have the same moon, stars and cherry blossoms that Issa saw and celebrated all his life.

Some swallows coming up now. Follow me on my wanderings. This time to Morroco:

snails in their soup
and swallows dancing—
dancing in the firmament

Way to go! Above-below, darting like a swallow. And now to Egypt:

Valley of the Kings
plastic bottles that will last
a thousand years

The Nile in the evening
the silence of extinct
crocodiles

Here's one from Valparaiso, in Chile. Can you find it on the map?

flea-market in Valparaiso
a German helmet
rusting away

But for the haikuist, there's no place like home. If you are lucky enough to have a garden, well then, that's all you need:

thrush
on the lawn
daisy inspector

Some people might class this as a *senryu* rather than a haiku. And the next one too:

how noble!
the horse on a coin
no longer currency

A question! What's the connection between Anglo-Irish poet William Butler Yeats and the horse that's depicted on that coin? There's a project for you! Animals and birds on stamps and coins.

Before the euro, there were many different animals inscribed on the coins of Ireland: the hen and her brood, the salmon, bull, hound, hare, wren and many others. No tadpole, however!

alone tonight
with tadpoles—
with the universe

The tadpoles were there in large numbers and overhead the night-sky was decorated with stars. I didn't mention the stars.

You can't mention everything. After all, it's just three lines. But it's one of those above-below, below-above experiences that happens when you have the haiku rocket-engine to lift you to the stars.

I've written many haiku about tadpoles (unknown to them) over the years. I even painted a haiku about tadpoles on the garden wall at home:

> the tadpoles
> are all awake
> let's wake up too!

Written originally in Irish, at one stage this became a morning call for my children whenever they slept late. Our children have grown. Tadpoles turn into frogs:

> baby frog! who was your mother
> where is she now?
> Autumn evening

We had a garden full of frogs at one time. Some of them were playful enough, others curious, some of them loners. If you think all frogs are the same, then have a good look at them again next time you see a few.

I wrote the following *senryu* while walking over the Halfpenny Bridge in Dublin city:

reflected
in the blind man's glasses—
sunset

You don't have much time to capture a haiku moment. Now, I'm a slow walker. In fact, I must be one of the slowest walkers in the whole of Europe! I could win a Slow Walking Competition except that I think there's enough competitiveness in the world as it is. Walk too fast and you'll miss things, such as snails, or walk over them. Anyway, how much time did I have to compose this haiku that day? A couple of seconds. That's all. In another few seconds the sun would be gone, no longer visible in the blind man's spectacles. I would have been unable to tune into an above-below moment.

One morning early, in Kochi (Cochin), India, I wrote this haiku:

Allāhu Akbar
first light over Kochi
trembling waves

I wrote a short essay called *Anatomy of a Haiku*, in an attempt to explain it to those who simply don't 'get' haiku. I was up at five o'clock to catch an early-morning flight. Opening a window, the first glimmer of dawn coincided with the muezzin's call to prayer. One doesn't like to read too much into anything but for the sake of elucidation, let's ask ourselves how many strands are at work here?

Firstly the muezzin cries out that God is Great. The emerging light of dawn is linked with this statement, physically and metaphysically. Already, sound and sight are weaving something new in my brain, a moment hitherto unexperienced... the invisible muezzin, his nameless voice. Light is becoming visible above the city and the muezzin's cry also comes from above so, without knowing it at the time, an above-below moment was happening!

Syllabically, this haiku amounts to fourteen syllables, the second line being the longest; this is more or less the favoured make-up of today's free-style haiku. Apart from Arabic, it's in plain enough language, wouldn't you say? It describes an event in time and space. Time of day often replaces the previous requirement of a *kigo* or seasonal reference.

It is reasonably euphonious, I hope, without being over-musical. So far so good with our rudimentary analysis. Those 'trembling waves' ... what might they be? 'Trembling waves' must obviously refer to waves on the sea. Kochi, after all, is a port city. A typical device which a haikuist often draws upon without intentionality, is to introduce a complementary image which resonates with the first, though not necessarily with any obvious association. (Many authors believe that such a device is, indeed, essential: see *The Poetics of Japanese Verse*, Koji Kawamoto, University of Tokyo Press 2000.)

'Waves' could also refer to sound waves, the voice of the muezzin. Or 'waves' might also refer to waves of light, light waves of the dawn. The waves of creation itself? Echoes of the Big Bang? Now now! Let's get a hold of ourselves here!

Yes, one can explain, in a logical or intuitive manner, in hindsight, things which were mysteriously and seamlessly one at the time of realizing the haiku moment, or its composition some time later in words. But isn't the Big Bang going a wee bit too far? Not really. Doesn't astronomy and cosmic physics teach us that compression leads, ultimately, to unbelievable expansion? And what is haiku but compression *par excellence*? (And if I am overstating my case, it's simply as an antidote to the reaction of those who dismiss the genre and see nothing at all in a haiku.) And 'trembling'? 'Trembling' could suggest something of the fear of God, God's greatness, proclaimed in the haunting voice that cuts through the early morning stillness. But, as it was written at the start of 2004, is there not the possibility that—subconsciously at least—'trembling' also suggests the pathological fear of Muslim culture which has become part of our world's neurosis today?

Or is 'trembling waves' nothing more than pathetic fallacy, a much-used device in Gaelic poetry? Is it the "I" that trembles? Before what? Itself? Before the power of monotheism? If so, what spurs this trembling? Fear? Loathing? Alienation? Ineffable admiration and awe?

I give these possible meanings—and allow for more—with the express intention of showing that a real haiku—as opposed to a pseudo-haiku—is not a slight thing at all. Much bad writing over the years has imprinted the haiku in popular imagination as nothing more than an amusing squib. We know it can be more than that, much more. It's up to the reader to complete the jigsaw with his or her own understanding and experience of what is real. Of course, I was not conscious of all these various levels and interpretations when the actual event happened. I was drawn into a web of sound, into tendrils of light, disappearing in their little gaps.

I'll leave you now with two haiku, each in different ways an above-below event:

crows over Clonmacnoise
their wing beats
bringing the darkness down

I make no secret of my love for crows! Does that mean I have no time for scarecrows?

with his one good hand
the scarecrow points
to the moon

Gabriel Rosenstock is a poet, haikuist, novelist, playwright for stage, TV and radio, short story writer, essayist and translator. His English-language haiku are collected in the book *Where Light Begins* (2012). Two books about haiku as a way of life were published by Cambridge Scholars Publishing in 2009: *Haiku Enlightenment* and *Haiku, the Gentle Art of Disappearing*. He has taught haiku at the Schule für Dichtung (Poetry Academy), Vienna, at the Hyderabad Literature Festival in India and at various venues in Ireland. His work has appeared in many key anthologies, most recently in *World Haiku Anthology on War, Violence and Human Rights Violation* (Kamesan Books 2013) and the ground-breaking anthology *Haiku in English: The First Hundred Years* (W.W. Norton & Co., 2013)

The Invisible Light is a book of photography by American master photographer Ron Rosenstock (no relation) with Gabriel's haiku in Irish, English, Spanish and Japanese. He is an Associate of the Haiku Foundation and a Charter Member of the Haiku & Tanka Society.

His blog: **http://roghaghabriel.blogspot.ie**

Mícheál Ó hAodha works at the University of Limerick. He has published many books in Irish and English. He is a regular contributor on arts and culture for the Irish-language columns of *The Irish Times* and also writes for the *Dublin Review of Books, An tUltach, Feasta, Beo.ie* etc. Some of his translations from the Irish appeared in the short story collection *Twisted Truths: Stories from the Irish* (2011) (Preface: Colm Tóibín). Two recent books are *Irish Migrants in New Communities: Seeking the Fair Land?* (ed. with Máirtín Ó Catháin), London: Rowman (2014) and *New Perspectives on the Irish Abroad: The Silent People?* (ed. with Máirtín Ó Catháin); London: Rowman (2014). His next book is due to be published shortly with Irish Academic Press.